Project Body

THE PROJECT MAKERS

John Farndon

WINDMILL BOOKS™

Published in 2020 by Windmill Books, an imprint of Rosen Publishing
29 East 21st Street, New York, NY 10010

Copyright © 2020 Miles Kelly Publishing

Publishing Director: Belinda Gallagher
Creative Director: Jo Cowan
Editorial Director: Rosie Neave
Senior Editor: Sarah Parkin
Designers: Joe Jones, Andrea Slane
Consultant: Steve Parker
Indexer: Jane Parker
Image Manager: Liberty Newton
Production: Elizabeth Collins, Jennifer Brunwin-Jones
Reprographics: Stephan Davis
Assets: Lorraine King

Cataloging-in-Publication Data

Names: Farndon, John.
Title: Project body / John Farndon.
Description: New York : Windmill Books, 2020. | Series: The project makers
| Includes index.
Identifiers: ISBN 9781538392232 (pbk.) | ISBN 9781725393028 (library bound)
| ISBN 9781538392249 (6 pack)
Subjects: LCSH: Human physiology--Experiments--Juvenile literature.
| Human body--Experiments--Juvenile literature.
Classification: LCC QP37.F37 2019 | DDC 612.0072--dc23
Manufactured in the United States of America

CPSIA Compliance Information: Batch #BW20WM:
For Further Information contact Rosen Publishing,
New York, New York at 1-800-237-9932

How to use the projects

This book is packed full of amazing facts about the human body. There are also 11 cool projects, designed to make the subject come alive.

Before you start a project:

• Always ask an adult to help you.

• Read the instructions carefully.

• Gather all the supplies you need.

• Clear a surface to work on and cover it with newspaper.

• Wear an apron or old T-shirt to protect your clothing.

Notes for helpers:

• Children will need supervision for the projects, usually because they require the use of scissors, or preparation beforehand.

• Read the instructions together before starting and help to gather the equipment.

IMPORTANT NOTICE
The publisher and author cannot be held responsible for any injuries, damage, or loss resulting from the use or misuse of any of the information in this book.

SAFETY FIRST!
Be careful when using glue or anything sharp, such as scissors.

How to use:
If your project doesn't work the first time, try again – just have fun!

HOW TO USE

Pinch the diaphragm plastic between your fingers and push firmly up inside the bottle. What happens to the lung balloon?

Pull the diaphragm plastic out to its fullest extent. Now what happens?

You should see the lung balloon inflate and deflate, as your lungs do when your diaphragm pulls.

Supplies:
The equipment should be easy to find, around the house or from a craft store. Always ask before using materials from home.

Numbered stages:
Each stage of the project is numbered and the illustrations will help you. Follow the stages in the order shown to complete the project. If glue or paint is used, make sure it is dry before moving on to the next stage.

Model lungs

Make your own working model of your lungs and diaphragm!

SUPPLIES

empty plastic water bottle • craft knife • balloon
• plastic bag • scissors • rubber band

HOW TO MAKE

1. Ask an adult to help you cut the top half off the bottle, keeping your cut straight. This will be your chest cavity.

2. Slip a balloon over the bottle's nozzle and push the balloon upside down firmly into the bottleneck. This is your lung.

3. Cut a square from the plastic bag that will cover the cut end of your bottle with a few centimeters to spare all around.

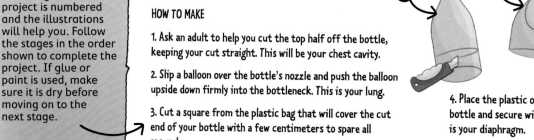

4. Place the plastic over the cut end of the bottle and secure with the rubber band. This is your diaphragm.

CONTENTS

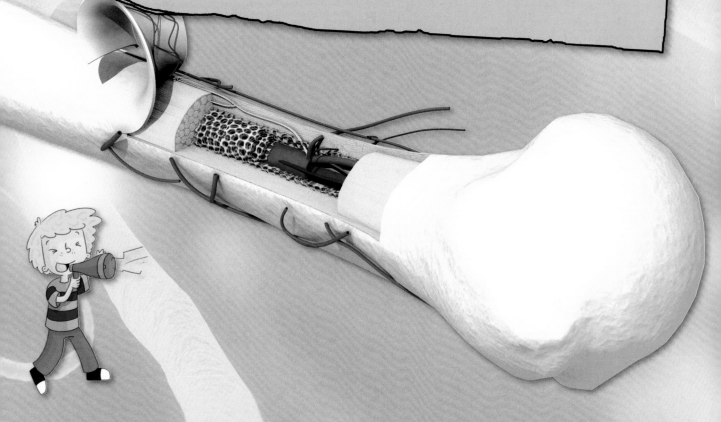

OUTSIDE IN

Together, your skin, hair, and nails are known as the integumentary system. Skin is waterproof, and shields you from infection. It's also your body's largest sense organ, providing your brain with vital data about the world.

SKIN SANDWICH

Although it's very thin, your skin is complicated. It has three main layers. The outer layer is made mostly of dead skin, and is called the epidermis (1). Beneath this, the dermis (2) contains all the glands and makes new skin cells. The innermost layer is mostly fat, and is called the hypodermis (3).

SUPER SURFACE

Your skin is just .08 of an inch (2 mm) thick on average, but it is so important that it receives up to one third of your body's blood supply and has its own special glands (organs that make chemical substances). It is waterproof, protects you against some of the harmful effects of sunlight, and helps keep you at just the right temperature. Skin even helps to nourish you by using sunlight to make vitamin D, and storing water, fat, glucose, and vitamin D.

Like apes and monkeys, we have a nail on the end of each of our fingers and toes. Nails are like the claws of other animals.

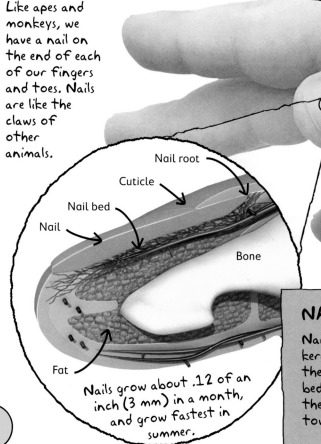

Nail root

Cuticle

Nail bed

Nail

Bone

Fat

Nails grow about .12 of an inch (3 mm) in a month, and grow fastest in summer.

Skin is thinnest on your eyelids, at just .02 inch (0.5 mm) thick, and thickest on the soles of your feet, where it is .2 inch (6 mm) thick.

NAILED IT

Nails are made from a tough material called keratin. They are mostly dead cells, except at the nail root where they are made, and the nail bed where they slide along the fingertip. As they grow, each whole nail is pushed along towards the tip of your finger.

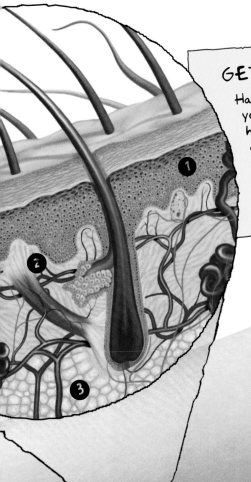

GETTING HAIRY

Hair is the fastest-growing thing on your body. You have about 100,000 hairs on your head, all growing about one centimeter per month, and hot weather makes them grow faster! People with fair hair have lots more hairs than those with red hair – 150,000 to a redhead's 90,000.

How do wounds heal?

First, platelet cells rush to the wound to make blood **clot** (thicken and stick together).

Next, other special blood cells (white) arrive to fight **infection**.

Then material in the blood called **fibrin** (yellow) forms a fibrous mesh. Platelets and red blood cells are trapped. They form a jelly-like mass, which dries to form a **scab**, and the skin heals underneath.

Sun stoppers

Too much sun can damage your skin. Find out how well suntan lotions protect it with this simple test.

SUPPLIES

masking tape • scissors • transparent plastic folders • two or more sunscreens with the same protection factor • tray • sunprint paper kit • tub or basin of water

HOW TO MAKE

1. Stick the masking tape in a simple pattern onto the plastic folders (one for each lotion).

2. Smear a different sunscreen onto each folder. Label them so you can identify them.

3. Place one folder on a flat tray, slide a sheet of sunprint paper into it, take the tray out into the sun, and leave in direct sunlight for two minutes (or according to your kit's instructions).

4. Bring the tray back out of the sun, take the paper out of the folder, and immerse in water for one minute (or according to kit instructions), then lay flat to dry.

5. Repeat steps 3 and 4 for all your folders.

6. Check the strength of the patterns on the prints: the weakest pattern indicates the strongest sun protection.

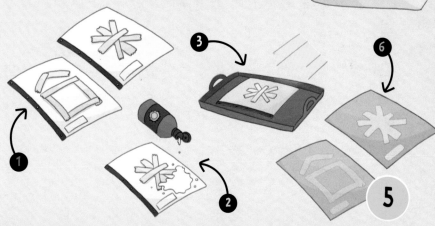

AIR BAGS

Every cell in your body needs a continual supply of oxygen — especially those in your brain. That's why your body has an incredible system for taking oxygen from the air when you breathe in, and why you would die if you stopped breathing.

BREATHTAKING

Inside your chest, you have two lungs. Each lung is a spongy bag packed full of tiny branching airways, like an upside-down tree. When you breathe in, your lungs inflate like balloons to draw air in through your nose and mouth and down your trachea (windpipe). Scientists call breathing respiration.

Your lungs take oxygen from the air into the blood vessels that surround them so that it can be pumped around your body by your heart.

Windpipe

Lung

Heart

BREATH POWER

Your blood delivers energy to your cells in the form of a sugary chemical called glucose. In the same way that a fire needs oxygen to burn, your cells need oxygen to release the energy from glucose. The process releases carbon dioxide, which your body expels as you breathe out, because it is poisonous.

When you run fast, your muscles need extra oxygen, so your lungs must work hard to take in more air.

Model lungs

Make you own working model of your lungs and diaphragm!

SUPPLIES

plastic water bottle • craft knife • balloon • plastic bag • scissors • rubber band

HOW TO MAKE

1. Ask an adult to help you cut the top half off the empty bottle, keeping your cut straight. This will be your chest cavity.

2. Slip a balloon over the bottle's nozzle and push the balloon upside down firmly into the bottleneck. This is your lung.

3. Cut a square from the plastic bag that will cover the cut end of your bottle with a few centimeters to spare all around.

4. Place the plastic over the cut end of the bottle and secure with the elastic band. This is your diaphragm.

HOW TO USE

Pinch the diaphragm plastic between your fingers and push firmly up inside the bottle. What happens to the lung balloon?

Pull the diaphragm plastic out to its fullest extent. Now what happens?

You should see the lung balloon inflate and deflate, as your lungs do when your diaphragm pulls.

It's a gas

1. You breathe in **air** containing oxygen (O_2) and other gases.

2. In the **lungs**, O_2 is taken into the bloodstream.

3. O_2 is carried away in the **blood**.

4. Blood carries carbon dioxide (CO_2) back to the **lungs**.

5. CO_2 is carried out of the body as you **breathe out**.

Bronchiole

The bronchi branch into tens of thousands of narrower pipes called bronchioles.

Bronchi

At the bottom of the windpipe, the airways fork into two large pipes called bronchi, one leading to each lung.

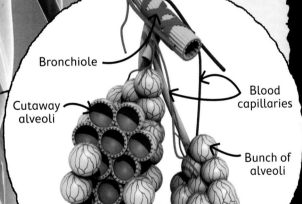

Bronchiole

Cutaway alveoli

Blood capillaries

Bunch of alveoli

Diaphragm

When you breathe in, your chest muscles and diaphragm (a large sheet of muscle beneath the lungs) pull out to make the lungs expand. When you breathe out, the muscles relax to let the lungs collapse like a deflated balloon.

PUMP IT!

Your heart is a pump that pushes blood around your body. It beats away inside your chest to keep blood constantly circulating. No cell in your body can survive long without the array of chemicals delivered in the blood.

Artery

BLOOD ON THE MOVE

One side of your heart pumps blood around your body through a branching network of tubes called blood vessels. It pumps bright-red blood rich in fresh oxygen away from the lungs through vessels called arteries. Once it has delivered its oxygen, the blood turns purple and returns to the heart through blood vessels called veins.

The red arteries and blue veins are like two similar branching trees of blood vessels, meeting at your heart.

Your heart beats about 70 times a minute and over **30 million times** each year. When you exert yourself, it beats **even faster**.

Your heart is a special muscle that contracts and expands entirely automatically

Blood groups

Your blood is one of four main groups. If you are injured and need to be given blood, you must receive blood from the right group, as your **immune system** may fight against blood from the wrong group.

The most common blood group is **O**. Blood from this group can be given safely to any other group. People with this blood type are known as **universal** donors.

The other **three** main blood groups are A, B, and AB.

BLOOD COCKTAIL

Blood looks red, but is mostly a yellowish fluid called plasma. The red comes from the red blood cells swept along in it. It also contains giant white cells called leucocytes and little lumps called platelets, plus salts, hormones, fats, and sugars.

Button-shaped red blood cells carry oxygen through the blood. Spiky, ball-shaped white blood cells help your body fight infection.

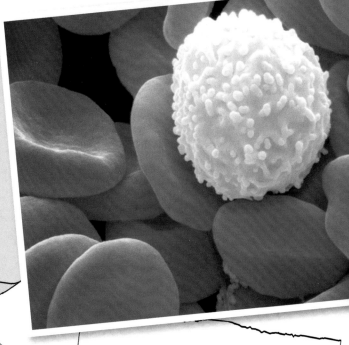

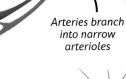

Arteries branch into narrow arterioles

Vein

Arterioles branch into tiny capillaries

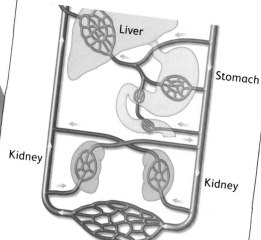

Liver

Stomach

Kidney

Kidney

This diagram shows the two parts of blood circulation. Blood rich in oxygen is red, deoxygenated blood is blue.

Listen to the beat

Doctors sometimes listen to your chest using a device called a stethoscope. Here's how to make a simple stethoscope to listen to your heart beating.

SUPPLIES

3 feet (1 m) of plastic tubing • plastic funnel

HOW TO MAKE

Insert the neck of the funnel into one end of the tube.

HOW TO USE

1. Hold the mouth of the funnel against your chest, slightly to your left. This is where your heart is. Put the other end of the tube against your ear and listen hard. You should hear your heart beating.

2. Run in place for a few minutes, then listen to your heart again – it should be beating faster.

DOWN THE HATCH

When you swallow food, it begins a long journey down through your gut. On its way, it is gradually broken down into chemical molecules small enough for your body to absorb and use. This breakdown process is called digestion.

Your stomach can swell up to **eight times** as big when it is full.

THE FOOD TUBE

Your gut is a very long tube that curls through your body between your mouth and your anus, around 33 feet (10 m) long. It's also called the alimentary canal and runs down through your gullet, your stomach, your small intestine, and your large intestine.

Your stomach produces hydrochloric **acid** strong enough to dissolve a lump of bone in a few hours. That's why your stomach lining is coated with protective mucus.

1

Your stomach is a bag-like organ, and it's where the breakdown of food really begins. Chemicals inside it attack the food, and the walls squeeze it to a pulp. Your stomach also stores partially digested food until the rest of the gut is ready to receive it.

Enzyme breakdown

Biological soap powders use special chemicals called enzymes to clean dirt proteins on clothes. You can use them to see how enzymes in your digestive system break down proteins in food.

SUPPLIES

jam • teaspoon • two strips of white cotton • small amount of biological soap power with enzymes and nonbiological soap powder without enzymes • two small dishes • water

HOW TO MAKE

1. Smear a patch of jam on each cotton strip and let them dry.

2. Mix a little of each soap in separate dishes with the same amount of water.

3. Dip the jammy part of one cotton strip into the dish containing the soap with enzymes and the other into the one without.

4. Leave the strips for half an hour. You should find the jam is almost gone from the strip in the enzyme dish. The enzymes break up the proteins in jam in the same way as enzymes in your gut break down proteins in food.

Esophagus

Liver

Stomach

Gallbladder

Large intestine

Small intestine

Bladder

3

Your small intestine is where food goes after it's mashed to a pulp in your stomach. As the food pulp passes through your small intestine, it is digested and absorbed into your body. Any indigestible food passes on into the large intestine. Here, water is soaked up, and the semidry waste is pushed out through your anus.

SUPER SURFACE

The inside of your small intestine is lined with countless tiny finger-like projections called villi. These help give a huge surface for food to be absorbed.

Food takes up to **24 hours** to pass through the gut.

0 hours: When you **swallow** food, it slides down to the stomach where it is broken down into semiliquid form.

06:00

4 hours: Partially digested food passes from the **stomach** to the small intestine.

10:00

7 hours: Broken-down food molecules are absorbed into the **bloodstream** in the second half of the small intestine.

01:00

9 hours: Undigested food passes into the large intestine, where any **water** is soaked up.

03:00

17–24 hours: Waste passes into the rectum and is then excreted up to **two days** later.

11:00

WATER WORKS

Besides food and air, your body needs water. You cannot survive more than a few days without it. Your body is more than 60 percent water, and the balance of water is crucial to your survival.

HOLDING WATER

When your body has too little water, the concentration of chemicals in your blood goes up. A special organ in your brain called the hypothalamus detects this, and sends a signal to another organ called the pituitary gland. The pituitary releases a chemical called ADH, which tells your kidneys to let less water escape as urine in order to restore the balance.

When you sweat to keep cool, your brain's hypothalamus (1) detects the water loss and tells the pituitary gland (2) to send out thirst signals.

Water Balance

The amount of water in your body must never vary by more than 5 percent. Constant adjustments – taking water in and letting it out – keep the balance just right.

Input	Pints
Drinks	2.5
Food	2
From body cells	0.5
TOTAL	5

Output	Pints
Urine	3
Sweat	1
Vapor in breath	0.6
Feces	0.4
TOTAL	5

FANTASTIC FILTERS

The main way you lose water is through urine, which is controlled by your kidneys. Your kidneys filter unwanted water from the blood and flush out waste chemicals. The waste water is then piped as urine into your bladder. There the pressure of liquid builds up until you urinate.

Every day, your kidneys filter 40 gallons (150 l) of blood and extract about 3 pints (1.5 l) of urine, which they expel through the ureter.

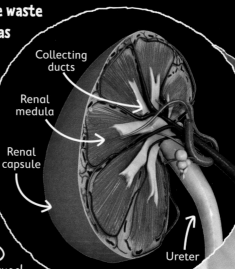

Collecting ducts

Renal medulla

Renal capsule

Ureter

The average human spends **6 months** on the toilet in a lifetime.

You urinate **11,890 gallons** (45,000 l) of water during your life – enough to fill a small **swimming pool**.

When pee is inside your body, it has no smell. But as soon as it comes out, the urea in pee begins to break down and smell.

Saving blood

To clean the blood, your kidneys must first filter out the larger particles it needs to save, such as blood cells and proteins. This experiment shows how filtering works.

SUPPLIES

jug • water • red food coloring • crushed chalk (about ½ tsp) • coffee filter • rubber band • large glass jar

HOW TO MAKE

1. Add about 150 ml of water to the jug.

2. Add a few drops of red food coloring and the chalk to the water.

3. Place the filter over the glass jar and secure with the rubber band so that it dips down into the jar by a few centimeters.

4. Slowly pour the colored water into the jar with the filter on top.

5. Notice how the filter traps the chalk while letting the colored water drip through. In the same way, your kidneys (the filter) let blood circulate while retaining the things they need to save (the chalk).

PULLING TOGETHER

Every move you make depends on muscles. You need them to go for a walk, chew your food, and even when you're fast asleep. Without them you'd just collapse like a puppet with its strings cut.

MUSCLE TYPES

You have two main kinds of muscles. Skeletal (voluntary) muscles cover your skeleton and allow you to move. Involuntary muscles work automatically to control body functions, such as your heartbeat.

Almost all of your 640 skeletal muscles are attached to your skeleton. They produce movement and give your body its shape.

1

2

3

6

4

7

5

8

Too cool! The strongest muscle in your body is the masseter muscles in your **cheeks** that make you bite. Your tongue is a close second.

The smallest muscle is less than .01 inch (1.3 mm) long. It's called the stapedius and is in your **inner ear.**

The largest muscles are made from **hundreds** of bundles of muscle fiber.

The biggest muscle is in your **bum.** It's called the gluteus maximus and gets its name from the Greek and Latin words for bum and biggest.

POWER CONTRACT

Muscles get their power from bundles of fibers that contract and relax. Inside each fiber are alternating, interlocking filaments of two substances called actin and myosin. These pull and twist into each other to shorten the muscle whenever they get a signal from the brain.

This microscope picture shows a slice across the tiny fibers of a muscle that give it its pulling power.

WORKING ...

A single muscle can only pull, not push. [E] time one muscle contracts, it must be pulled back to its original length by another muscle shortening in the opposite direction. This is why muscles are usually arranged in pairs.

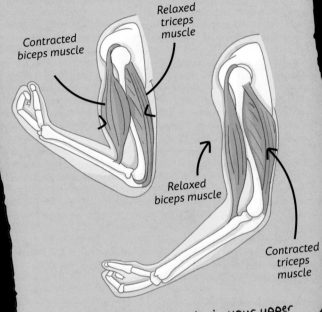

Contracted biceps muscle

Relaxed triceps muscle

Relaxed biceps muscle

Contracted triceps muscle

The biceps and triceps muscles in your upper arm work in conjunction to pull your forearm one way then the other.

MUSCLES OF THE ARMS AND TORSO

1 Trapezius
2 Deltoid
3 Pectoralis
4 Biceps
5 Triceps
6 Brachioradialis
7 Rectus abodominis
8 External oblique abdominal

MUSCLES OF THE LEGS

9   Adductors
10 Pectineus
11 Tensor fasciae latae
12 Sartorius
13 Rectus femoris
14 Vastus lateralis
15 Vastus medialis
16 Tibialis anterior
17 Gastrocnemius
18 Soleus

If all the muscles in your body **pulled together** they [could lift a bus!]

BONE IDOL

Bones give your body a strong, rigid, but remarkably light framework called the skeleton. Inside, bones are crisscrossed by a super-strong combination of flexible collagen fibers and stiff honeycomb-like struts called trabeculae.

All about joints

Swivel joints in the neck allow the head to rotate.

The **saddle** joint allows your thumb to move in two directions.

Ellipsoidal joints, found at the base of the first finger and in the toes, allow movement in various directions.

Ball-and-socket joints, found in the hip and shoulder, allow circular movement.

Hinge joints, like those in the elbow and knee, allow a swinging movement to and fro.

Plane joints in the wrists and ankles allow smooth circular and bending movements.

Many of the bones in your body are long and thin. Exceptions include the hipbones (or pelvis) and the skull.

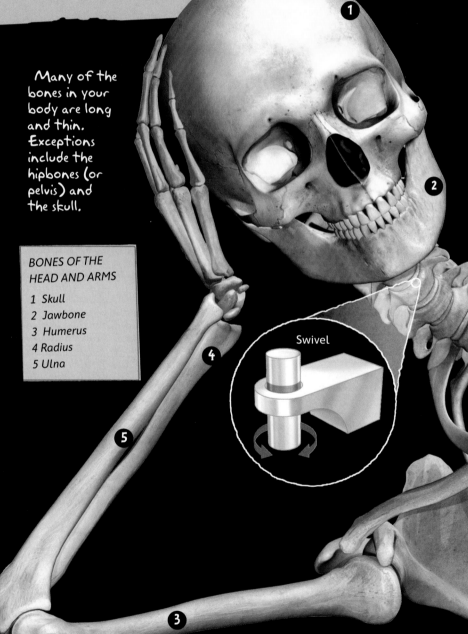

BONES OF THE HEAD AND ARMS

1 Skull
2 Jawbone
3 Humerus
4 Radius
5 Ulna

Swivel

Weight for weight, **bone** is five times as strong as **steel**.

More than **half** the bones in your body are in your **hands** and **feet**. There are 26 bones in each foot, linked by 33 muscles.

LIVING BONES

Your skeleton is the one part of your body that remains long after you die. Yet while you're alive, it's living tissue, packed inside with cells called osteocytes between the framework of hard minerals.

Bone has a hard cortex of compact bone encasing spongy cancellous bone. In the middle is a soft core or marrow.

Marrow and blood vessels

Hard cortex or compact bone

Spongy or cancellous bone

Periosteum (outer covering)

SUPER SKELETON

Your skeleton is made of over 200 bones. It has two main parts. The axial skeleton is the core of the skeleton. It's basically the skull, spine, and ribcage. The appendicular skeleton is all the other bones that are attached to this, including the shoulders, arms, hands, hips, legs, and feet.

The soft, spongy center or marrow of the breastbone, ribs, and hips are factories for **new blood cells.**

9

10

Saddle

BONES OF THE BACK AND CHEST
6 Collarbone
7 Breastbone
8 Ribs
9 Spine
10 Hip bone

A gymnast's muscles pull the bones to which they are anchored so that they can perform a range of movements requiring supreme flexibility, balance, control, and strength.

JOINT ENTERPRISE

The skeleton is strong and rigid, yet can bend pretty much any way you want. That's because it's made of lots of separate bones linked only by movable joints. Here, the bones are held together by fibers called ligaments and cushioned by smooth, rubbery cartilage.

There are **80 bones** in the axial skeleton and **126 bones** in the appendicular skeleton.

Ball-and-socket

STUDYING THE SKELETON

The first accurate drawings of the skeleton were made by Johannes Stephanus of Calcar in the 1540s. He drew the bones of bodies that had been carefully dissected (cut up) by the famous Belgian physician Andre Vesalius. The skeleton Vesalius prepared can still be seen in Basel in Switzerland.

Calcar's drawings showed intricate details of anatomy, often in poses like this one, which shows a skeleton as if relaxing against a tomb.

11

12

BONES OF THE
HIP AND LEGS

11 Thigh bone
12 Kneecap
13 Shinbone
14 Calf bone

Hinge

Bone is so light it accounts for only **14 percent** of total body weight.

Bone can stand being squeezed twice as hard as **granite** and being stretched four times as hard as **concrete**.

BROKEN BONES

Sometimes, despite their strength, bones do get broken or fractured. Fortunately, most fractures heal. First, the body stops any bleeding, then gradually the fracture is knitted together with new bone by osteoblasts. But surgeons may need to straighten the break out and hold it in place with pins or a plaster cast to ensure the bone repairs itself in the right way.

When bones break this badly, they must be realigned by surgery to heal properly.

The word skeleton comes from the **ancient Greek** word for dry.

Ellipsoidal

13

14

Plane

19

BRILLIANT BRAIN

If you could see your brain, you might say it looks like a giant gray walnut. But it's actually the most amazing structure, containing hundreds of billions of nerve cells, some of them linked to 25,000 or more others, creating trillions of connections.

INSIDE YOUR BRAIN

Your brain is 85 percent water and quite a lot of fat. But what really matters is the nerve cells held in tight bundles by supporting glial cells. The brain is split into two hemispheres, linked by a bundle of nerves. Scientists can learn about the brain by studying MRI scans – images made using strong magnetic fields to show details of brain structure and activity.

The inside of your brain is much more than just a dense mat of fibers. Inside is a variety of structures, each with its own task.

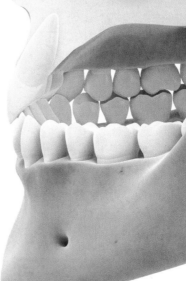

CORTEX →
The wrinkled outer layer is where your brain receives all the sense signals from your body and responds with messages to react.

Where's that letter?

You can test how good your short-term memory is with this simple word game. You can use letters from a game, or you can make your own paper letter tiles.

HOW TO PLAY

1. Select 16 letter tiles – start with eleven consonants and five vowels, and make sure you have a good variety of letters.

2. Lay them on a flat surface in a grid, face up. Try to memorize the position of each letter.

3. Turn all the letters facedown.

4. Turn one letter faceup. Using your memory, see if you can turn over tiles in the right order to form a word of at least three letters.

5. Once you have made a word, try to make a second.

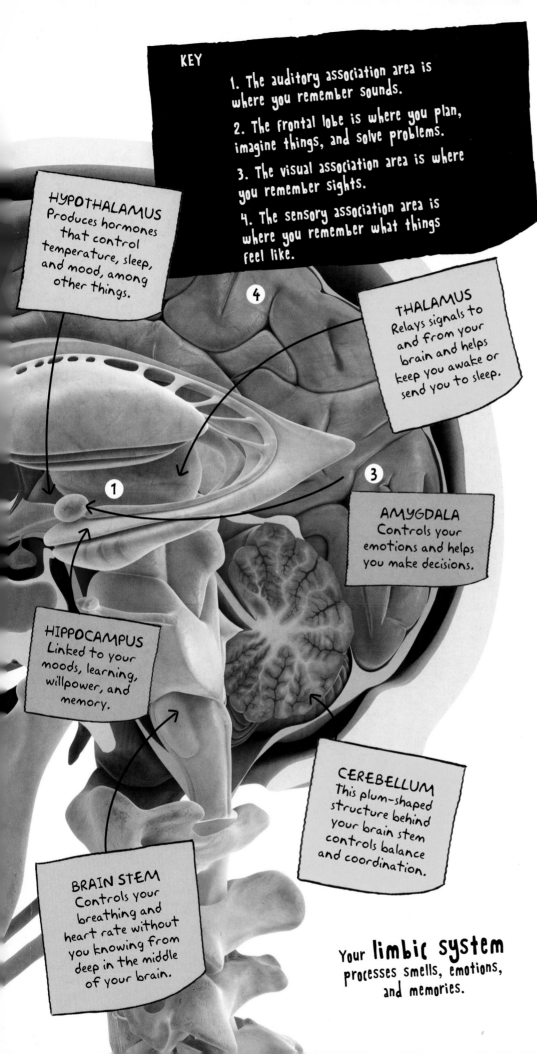

1. The auditory association area is where you remember sounds.

2. The frontal lobe is where you plan, imagine things, and solve problems.

3. The visual association area is where you remember sights.

4. The sensory association area is where you remember what things feel like.

HYPOTHALAMUS
Produces hormones that control temperature, sleep, and mood, among other things.

THALAMUS
Relays signals to and from your brain and helps keep you awake or send you to sleep.

AMYGDALA
Controls your emotions and helps you make decisions.

HIPPOCAMPUS
Linked to your moods, learning, willpower, and memory.

CEREBELLUM
This plum-shaped structure behind your brain stem controls balance and coordination.

BRAIN STEM
Controls your breathing and heart rate without you knowing from deep in the middle of your brain.

Your **limbic system** processes smells, emotions, and memories.

I remember

Your brain stores **memories** by making new connections between brain cells. They are made in three stages:

1. Sensory
memory: Your senses continue seeing, hearing, or feeling something for a short while after it stops.

2. Short-term
memory: Your brain stores something like a name just long enough to pass it on.

3. long-term
memory: Your brain makes strong connections so that you remember things for a long time.

3a. Declarative memories are things you remember **consciously**, such as the name of your favorite band or where the supermarket is.

3b. Non-declarative memories are things you remember **subconsciously**, such as how to tie your shoelaces.

GET THE MESSAGE

Your nervous system is your body's control system. It's like a high-speed internet, with neurons (nerve cells) whizzing messages to and fro. Sensory neurons receive messages from the senses, while motor neurons send messages to the muscles to move.

NERVE CENTRAL

The hub of your nervous system is the bundle of nerves running down your spine, known as the spinal cord. Together with your brain it makes up the central nervous system (CNS). More nerves branch out from the CNS all over the body. These nerves are the peripheral nervous system (PNS). Sensory neurons transmit nerve impulses from sensory receptors to the CNS. Motor neurons transmit signals from the CNS, telling the muscles to move.

Nerves branch out all over the body from the central nervous system, which consists of the brain and the spinal cord.

Brain

The **fastest** nerve signals travel at 394 feet (120 m)/sec!

Spinal cord

Intercostal nerve

Sciatic nerve

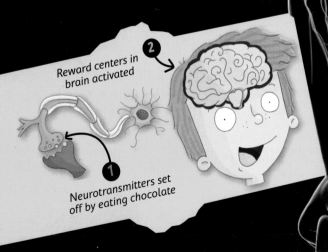

Reward centers in brain activated **2**

Neurotransmitters set off by eating chocolate **1**

MAKING A CONNECTION

Neurons transmit signals through a combination of electrical and chemical pulses. They receive signals from other neurons through thousands of branching connectors called dendrites. They send signals out via an axon (a long tail) to lots more dendrites, which are linked to other neurons.

After passing a signal, a nerve cell is ready to send another in 0.01 second!

MIND THE GAP

No two nerve cells touch. Instead, they transmit signals across a synapse (a tiny gap), in the form of neurotransmitters (streams of chemical particles). Nerve cells respond in different ways to different neurotransmitters, so these can have a dramatic effect on your mood.

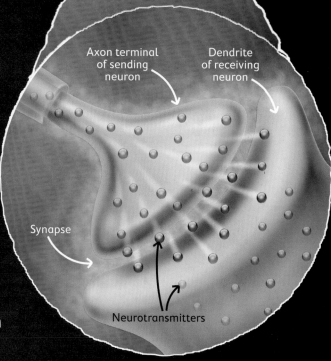

Axon terminal of sending neuron

Dendrite of receiving neuron

Synapse

Neurotransmitters

Test your reflexes

Reflex movements are muscle movements in your body that happen without you thinking about them. An alarm signal from a sense neuron goes straight to a motor neuron, cutting your brain out of the process so that your body can react with lightning speed.

HOW TO DO:

1. Ask a friend to sit cross-legged so that one leg dangles freely.

2. Tap his or her leg firmly with the side of your hand just below the kneecap.

3. If you hit the right place, your friend's leg will kick out immediately.

HOW IT WORKS

The tap makes the thigh muscle stretch. In 50 milliseconds, the information is sent to the spinal cord, and then comes straight back to the thigh muscle to make it contract and kick out your leg.

ALL EYES

Eyes are sometimes compared to cameras. But their picture quality beats even the best digital cameras. They are also much more versatile than any camera – they can focus on a speck of dust just inches away or a galaxy far across the universe, and work in both starlight and sunlight.

The **iris** is what gives you the **color** of your eyes.

The pupil looks dark because the eye is dark inside

The cornea is a dish-shaped lens at the front of the eye and is as clear as glass

The iris widens and narrows to control the amount of light entering the eye

EYE EYE

Your eyes are two hollow balls with a round window at the front called the pupil. Each is filled with a jelly-like substance called vitreous humor. Vitreous means glass-like and humor means body fluid.

The ciliary muscles adjust the shape of the lens so it can focus at different distances

The lens is a secondary, adjustable lens behind the cornea

Each of your eyes sees things from a slightly different angle. Your brain combines the two different views to give an impression of depth and solidity rather than just a flat picture.

The lens (towards the top of this illustration) contains a vast number of cells. Jelly-like vitreous humor in the main body of the eye holds they eye's shape and keeps everything in place.

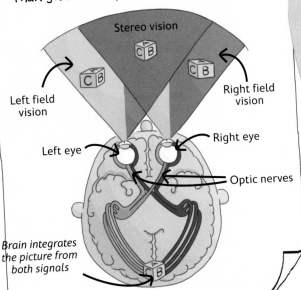

Stereo vision

Left field vision

Right field vision

Left eye

Right eye

Optic nerves

Brain integrates the picture from both signals

The optic nerve carries signals from the retina to your brain

24

Make a stereoscope

Our brain combines two pictures – one from each eye – to give us our view of the world. The difference between the angles of the two is what gives everything a solid, 3-D look. A simple stereoscopic viewer can mimic this 3-D view.

SUPPLIES

digital camera – one on a phone is fine ● computer ● photoprint paper ● printer ● scissors ● tape ● an old shoebox

HOW TO MAKE

1. Support the camera on a table or window ledge, then take a picture.

2. Slide the camera about 4 inches (10 cm) sideways and take a second picture of the same thing.

3. Load the pictures onto a computer and print them. They must be small enough to sit side by side, a few millimeters apart at one end of your box. Cut them out and tape them inside the box, as shown.

4. Cut the lid of the shoebox down to a size where it can form a central divider along the length of your box. Use tape to hold it in place.

5. Cut eyeholes in the box at the opposite end to your pictures.

HOW TO USE

Look through the viewing holes. The two photos will seem to merge, giving your brain the impression that you are looking at a single 3-D object. You may need to experiment with how far away from your eyes you hold the box, to find the right position.

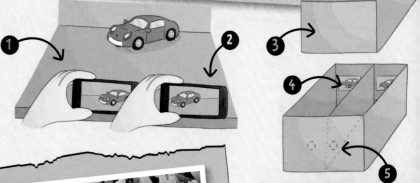

When light hits the retina, the rods and cones send nerve signals down the optic nerve to the visual cortex in the brain, creating your own private movie in your head.

The retina is a mass of light sensor cells that carpet the back of the eye

This hugely magnified picture shows the rods (white) and cones (green) in the eye's retina.

YOUR OWN CAMERA

The picture in your eye is millimeters across, yet seems so big and real you never think of it as a picture. The retina that picks it up is like an array of photocells. Rods – 130 million of them – detect if it's dark or light, and work even in low light; 8 million cones detect colors and work best in daylight.

Too cool!

Your eyes can tell the difference between **8 million** different colors.

You blink 10–24 times a minute – that's **415 million** times in a lifetime.

You have **200 eyelashes** on each eye to protect them from dust.

SOUND SYSTEM

Your ears are fantastically sensitive devices for picking up the tiny vibrations in the air that make sound. Your pinnae (ear flaps) are just the funnels to send the vibrations on to the pickup devices inside your head.

EAR WE GO

Your ear has three sections. The outer ear is the ear flap and ear canal (the tunnel into your head), where sounds are collected. In the middle ear, sound waves are turned into vibrations. The inner ear is where the vibrations are detected.

Super sound waves

Here's a simple project to show how sounds affect your ears so that you hear them.

SUPPLIES

plastic wrap • large bowl • uncooked rice (any other small grain will work) • tin lid (or other noisemaker)

HOW TO MAKE

1. Stretch the plastic wrap tightly over the bowl to make your ear drum model.

2. Scatter some rice grains on the plastic wrap.

3. Firmly hold the tin lid close to your "eardrum" and bang the lid with your hand. Watch the rice grains move and even jump.

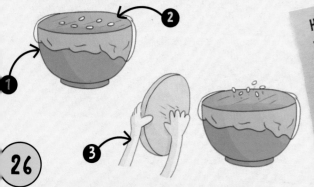

HOW IT WORKS

The bang generates sound waves that make the plastic sheet vibrate and causes the rice grains to move. Sound waves vibrate the eardrum in much the same way.

Every sound you hear is funneled down the ear canal into the mechanism of the middle and then inner ear. The middle ear turns the changes in air pressure made by sound waves into vibrations that can be detected by your aural (hearing) nerves.

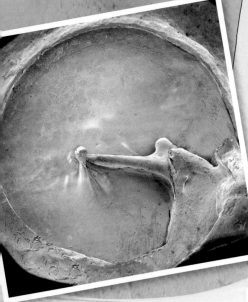

BANG THE DRUM

In your middle ear, sounds hit the eardrum (a thin wall of skin), causing it to vibrate. As it vibrates it rattles the ossicles (three tiny bones), amplifying the vibration.

The pink in this microscope picture shows the eardrum from the inside. The hammer bone is just touching it.

PASS IT ALONG

The vibration in the ossicles starts with the hammer. This shakes the anvil so it bangs against the stirrup. The stirrup then knocks against the cochlea – a fluid-filled tube shaped like a snail's shell.

Eardrum

The three bones of the ossicle have names connected with the craft of the blacksmith.

STEADY!

Your ears are what keep you from falling over. Next to the cochlea is a cluster of three fluid-filled rings called semicircular canals. These canals act like tiny levels, telling you when you're tilting one way or another as the fluid moves inside the canal.

A climber's balance depends on a combination of the fluid-filled canals in his ears and sensors in joints and muscles all over his body.

SUPER SENSES

Your senses tell you all about the world. Besides sight and sound, there are taste, touch, and smell, and a host of other sensations from receptors all over your body.

Your brain uses nerve signals from a range of sensors to experience flavors. These sensors include taste buds in your tongue, aroma sensors in your nose, and others that detect qualities like texture and solidity.

UP YOUR NOSE

The olfactory cells in your nose work in much the same way as taste buds, but instead of five basic types, there are 350 or so! Different aromas stimulate different combinations of smell cells. The average person can identify over 10,000 smells.

Proprioceptors are sensors in joints and muscles all over your body that tell your brain about your **position** and **posture**. That's how you can touch your nose, even with your eyes closed.

WHAT A MOUTHFUL!

A food's flavor doesn't just depend on which of the taste buds in your tongue it triggers. It is also affected by its smell, its texture, and even how it looks! And not everyone tastes the same food the same way.

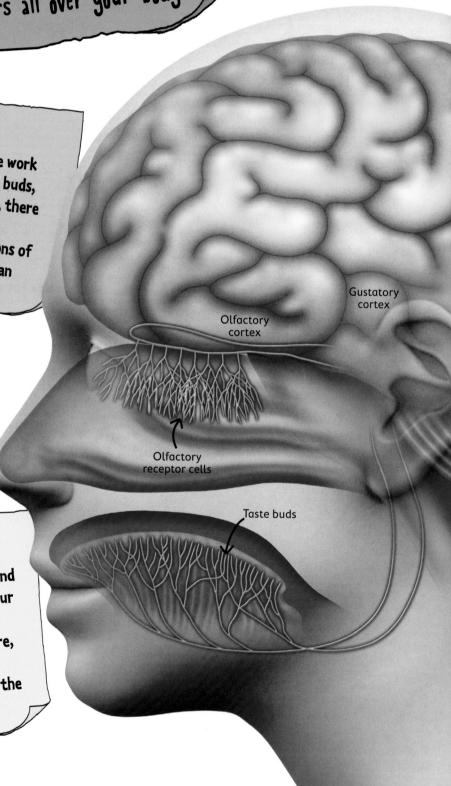

Gustatory cortex

Olfactory cortex

Olfactory receptor cells

Taste buds

Test your taste

Have you ever wondered why things don't taste much when you have a cold? When your nose is stuffed up, very little of the smell of your food can reach your olfactory center. This test shows what a difference your nose makes to what you can taste.

SUPPLIES
apple • potato • table knife • other fruits/vegetables

HOW TO DO

1. Cut an apple and a potato into small pieces of the same size.

2 Close your eyes, pinch your nose to block it, and lick one of the pieces. Can you tell what it is?

3. Try the other piece next.

4. Unblock your nose and try again. How do they taste now?

5. Try the same test for other foods.

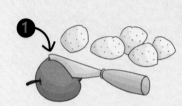

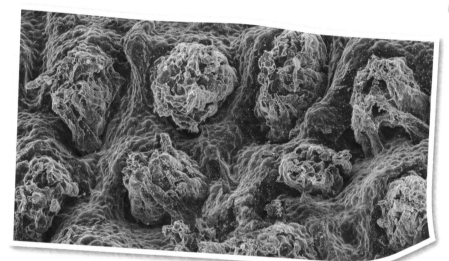

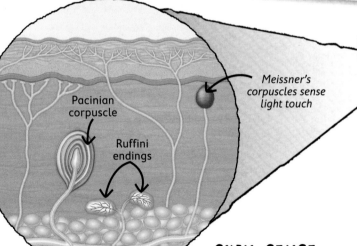

Meissner's corpuscles sense light touch

Pacinian corpuscle

Ruffini endings

SKIN SENSE

There are different receptors in your skin for pain, heat, cold, touch, and pressure. Some, called Pacinian corpuscles, respond quickly and then stop. Others, called Ruffini endings, respond slowly, then keep going.

Too cool!

Girls detect smells better than **boys**.

Your tongue can taste a **single drop** of lemon juice mixed in with 129,000 drops of water.

Your tongue has **8,000** taste buds.

Your fingertips are so sensitive they can feel an object move if it only moves one thousandth of a millimeter.

29

TO THE RESCUE!

Your body often comes under attack by disease-causing bacteria, viruses, and other germs. To fight these germs and keep you well, it has an array of biological weapons known as the immune system.

Body battles

Bacteria cause diseases such as whooping cough, tetanus, typhoid, and tuberculosis.

Viruses cause diseases such as colds and flu, mumps, rabies, and AIDS.

Allergy occurs when your body's defenses overreact to a particular intruder.

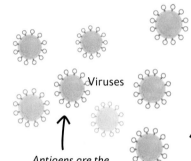

Viruses

Antigens are the tiny circles on the outside of each virus

Macrophage

As a macrophage engulfs a virus, antigens (traces of the virus) are left on its surface

T helper cells

1

Germs, such as viruses that enter the body, may be attacked by roving body cells called macrophages. Macrophages engulf a few viruses and kill them with toxic chemicals. Every germ has an identity tag on the outside called an antigen. When a macrophage engulfs a virus, it displays the virus's antigen on its surface.

2

White blood cells called T helpers have tags on their surface. If their tag matches the antigen on a macrophage, it locks on. Then it multiplies and sends out floods of chemicals that affect two more types of cells: B cells and T killers.

T killer cells

AT THE GATES

Your body has outer defenses to keep germs from getting in. The first barrier is your skin. And if germs sneak in through your nose and lungs as you breathe, they get bogged down in slimy mucus and blasted out with a cough or sneeze.

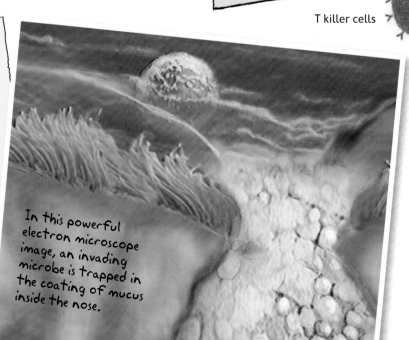

In this powerful electron microscope image, an invading microbe is trapped in the coating of mucus inside the nose.

Make fake mucus

Mucus is made mostly of sugars and protein. Although different than the ones found in the real thing, you can use sugars and protein to make fake mucus.

SUPPLIES

green food coloring • cup of water • tablespoon food supplement powder containing psyllium fiber • small plastic food box • microwave • spoon to stir

HOW TO MAKE

1. Add a few drops of food coloring to the cup of water.

2. Place 1 tbsp of fiber powder in the food box.

3. Add the water to the fiber powder and stir slowly but thoroughly.

4. Place the box in a microwave and heat for three minutes. Remove, stir briefly, and replace in the microwave for another two minutes.

5. Let your mucus cool before squeezing and stretching it – it should be fairly solid and very slimy. If it's still too liquid, you can put it back in the microwave for a minute more – the longer it cooks, the more solid it will become.

3

Meanwhile, viruses may have invaded some body cells. But the T killer cells can identify an infected cell by the virus antigens left on its surface. The killer locks on to the infected cell, floods it with toxic chemicals, and kills it.

There is a **different antibody** for every kind of germ.

B cells

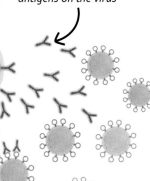

Plasma cell

Antibodies sent out by plasma cells lock onto matching antigens on the virus

Macrophage

4

When a B cell encounters a virus it recognizes, it reacts to the chemicals sent out by the T helper. Some B cells become plasma cells, which make and send out antibodies. The antibodies lock onto the matching antigens of the virus. Viruses marked with antibodies are at high risk of being engulfed by macrophages, and may also be damaged by the antibodies themselves.

INDEX

ACKNOWLEDGMENTS

The publishers would like to thank the following artists who have contributed to this book:

Julian Baker (J B Illustrations), Peter Bull (cover), Tom Heard (The Bright Agency) and Stuart Jackson-Carter

All other artwork from the Miles Kelly Artwork Bank

The publishers would like to thank the following sources for the use of their photographs:
t = top, b = bottom, l = left, r = right, c = center, m = main

Corbis 6(bl) Christian Charisius/dpa; 12–13(m) Mike Kemp/ Tetra Images

Glow 6–7(m) Pixologicstudio/Science Photo Library; 6(c) Sciepro/Science Photo Library; 11(bc) Sciepro/Science Photo Library; 22–23(m) Sciepro/Science Photo Library; 25(c) Steve Gschimeissner/Science Photo Library; 26–27(m) Science Picture Co/Superstock

Science Photo Library 5(c) Manfred Kage; 8–9(m) Pixologicstudio; 9(tr) Power and Syred; 10–11(m) Pixologicstudio; 15(c) Steve Gschmeissner; 20–21(m) Springer Medizin; 24–25(m) Jacopin/BSIP; 27(tl) Steve Gschmeissner, (c) DR Goran Bredberg; 29(c) Clouds Hill Imaging Ltd; 30(bc) Anatomical Travelogue; 31(cr) CDC

Shutterstock Cover(background) Sebastian Kaulitzki; 4–5(m) inxti; 18(tl) I T A L O; 18–19(t) Suzan Oschmann; 19(r) Praisaeng

Every effort has been made to acknowledge the source and copyright holder of each picture. Miles Kelly Publishing apologizes for any unintentional errors or omissions.